Let's Do The Numbers

Creating Your Retirement Income

Ian Sender
Former Director, Wall Street firms

IAN Books

An IAN Books paperback

Published by
IAN Books
41 Watchung Plaza, B242
Montclair, NJ 07042

Copyright © 2014 IAN Books

All rights reserved. No part of this book or its Interactive Internet CD can be reproduced, transmitted in any form or by any means, electronic or mechanical, including photocopying, recording, or by any information storage and retrieval system, without the written permission of the publisher.

Cover photo: la veille du début de la Semaine Olympique de Hyères 2005

Special sales for educational use by nonprofits.
IANBooksEditor@yahoo.com

ISBN-13: 978-1502775528

ISBN-10:1502775522

Library of Congress Control Number:2014918525

IAN Books at Amazon.com

Wealth Without Wall Street:
Buy Direct -- Avoid the Commissions, Fees, Loads

The Insiders' Guides to Buying Discount Financial Services:
Buy Direct and Save $3,000 Every Year

Drop Your Insurance:
Buy Only What You Need

Create Financial Freedom Using Your Wealth Reserve™:
Fix your financial life

The Simple Financial Life:
How to get what you want without going into debt and living paycheck to paycheck

Build Wealth Without Extra Money or Time:
You don't need to budget or get an extra job

Leah's Money Book:
"I want to control my own money."

The Working Millionaire:
$2,000,000 Tax-FREE Wealth Reserve ™ Self-insure Self-fund

Build Your Own $2,000,000 Tax-FREE Wealth Reserve™:
Self-insure Self-fund your lifestyle

Stop wasting $3,000 every year:
101
financial products ***NOT*** to buy and why

Long-term Care Insurance, *Updated 2013 Edition:*
Is it right for you? Are there better alternatives?

Contents

Spend $80,000 or $20,000 a year　　**Your Choice**　　5

1. $1,000,000 tax-FREE.　　11

2. One account.　　17

3. Compound high earnings.　　23

4. Automate contributions.　　27

5. Low-cost mutual funds.　　33

6. Global growth.　　39

7. Expenses less than income.　　45

8. Buy only services you need.　　49

9. Leave it alone.　　53

10. Tax-FREE income.　　57

Conclusion　　**Spend $80,000 or $20,000**　　61

The Author　　65

Spend $80,000 or $20,000 a year
Your choice

In my experience clients most satisfied with their retirement income were those that "did the numbers" themselves. They created the income level they enjoyed in retirement by working the numbers backward to determine how much to save and invest.

After estimating their Social Security and pension benefits, they decided they wanted $50,000 a year from investments. They knew that inflation would reduce their retirement dollar to fifty cents over time. That meant that they needed a nest egg of over $1 million in order to take $80,000 in future dollars ($50,000 current).

Since retirement plans (pensions and IRAs) allow money to compound WITHOUT taxes now, they used them at work and on their own. Younger clients have used Roth IRAs since it allows them to completely avoid income taxes on that money in time.

I showed these clients how to use a calculator to find the http://www.moneychimp.com/calculator/compound_interest_calculator.htm amount they needed to invest each year to reach their goal. You can reach $1 million in about 33 years by investing in low-cost stock market mutual funds inside a tax-FREE account. If you use a "managed" advisor/broker account, you earn less.

The average managed-investment account returns were 3.69% over the last 30 years according to a Dalbar QAIB study. During the same period your returns could have been over 11% if you had used low-cost stock-market index mutual funds. Your $250 monthly deposits would be worth $1,000,000 instead of $200,000.

Most "investors" are gamblers—buying a stock or mutual fund AFTER it has shown growth and then selling when the price falls. Buying and selling securities—"trading"—is NOT investing. Every time we buy and sell, it costs us a commission and fees. It costs us the gains the market made overall too. Salespeople make their living on the activity AND market gains. We keep ALL of the market's gains when we let a low-cost fund compound our returns.

Your financial sales person may be taking 63% of your

possible investment returns. Your employer's retirement plan may be taking over HALF your potential earnings. How much could you have earned in a low-cost stock market mutual fund during the last 20 years, 10 years or 5 years? Use this calculator to learn: http://www.moneychimp.com/features/market_cagr.htm

Fidelity just did a study of their client's 401k accounts. Those with over $1 million were long-term contributors. They did not trade and they did not cash out when they changed jobs. They invested for over 30 years. Their patience paid off.

How do we create $80,000 a year retirement income? We build a $1,000,000 account in about 33 years. We invest using the Buffett strategy: Compound high investment earnings. We earn money on the prior earnings of our money. Buffett turned $6,000 from paper routes into $60 billions by holding stocks "forever."

> "My wealth has come from a combination of living in America, some lucky genes, and **compound interest**."

Compounding works best when we keep our money at work in successful businesses paying dividends and stock splits, with no taxes or high fees. The table below gives us some idea of how fast our money can grow if we stay invested in businesses whose products we use every day.

Monthly	Accumulation at 12% per year									
	5	10	15	20	25	30	35	40	45	50
$100	$8,167	$23,004	$49,958	$98,925	$187,884	$349,496	$643,095	$1,176,477	$2,145,469	$3,905,834
$200	$16,334	$46,008	$99,916	$197,850	$375,768	$698,992	$1,286,190	$2,352,954	$4,290,938	$7,811,668
$300	$24,501	$69,012	$149,874	$296,775	$563,652	$1,048,488	$1,929,285	$3,529,431	$6,436,408	$11,717,502
$500	$40,835	$115,020	$249,790	$494,625	$939,420	$1,747,480	$3,215,475	$5,882,385	$10,727,346	$19,529,169

Investing is owning businesses for a long time. This kind of investment return is **possible but not guaranteed**. But wouldn't you rather have $1 million, more or less, than $200,000 in the bank? Investing is all about putting your money in businesses so that *over time* you can get back your money multiplied many times over. Buying and then selling a business is gambling. Wealthy people keep their money working in businesses.

Are you willing to spend $9 a day now for a tax-FREE future? You have an excellent chance of receiving $1,000,000 with

ZERO tax. I show you where to find the $250 a month on pages 49-52.

With this strategy, you invest in a number of successful businesses. If one fails, you will still earn 10-12% a year over time. You want to invest at little or no charge. That way your account could compound at the full 10-12%. Of course, you don't want to pay taxes. You want to invest a fixed amount like $250 or $500 a month (about $9 a day for each of you) so you don't miss a **stock sale**. Finally, you review your statement just once a year. I will show how to set up the best investing practices in only one hour.

Fortunately, low-cost mutual funds and tax-FREE trusts were invented in the last few years. You can now avoid Wall Street's fees of 1-3% and avoid taxes FOREVER. You can benefit from the FULL **power of compounding**. Many people like you have taken these steps to become wealthy over time. And now the steps have been made easier. You can do it yourself in an hour.

We can also save on taxes like the rich. Warren Buffett pays only 17% **total** tax. http://www.youtube.com/watch?v=Cu5B-2LoC4s. Mitt Romney and John Kerry pay less than 15%. We can use a special IRS-approved tax haven to protect all our investment earnings. We don't have to hide income in multilayer-corporate shells like Apple and Google. We **go tax-FREE** with our investment earnings. We pay 0% tax, adding an extra 25-30%.

Compounding works best if we do NOT have to pay tax on the earnings nor advisor fees every year. That way ALL of our earnings would be reinvested for the next period. This illustrates what happens to tax-FREE compounding over time.

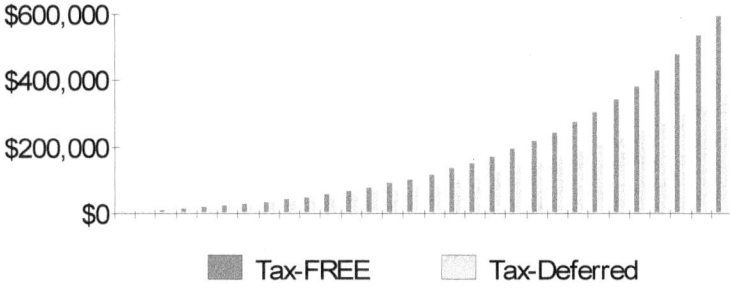

Tax-FREE v Taxable

For most working people, building a $1,000,000 fund takes patience and time. We become wealthy by investing in our own business or the businesses owned by the mutual funds we buy every month. We create wealth by waiting for our wealth to grow.

I have been in financial services for over 20 years. I ran sales organizations in several financial firms. Working directly and indirectly with clients helping them make a future was my job.

The key factor in building wealth is **maximizing the miracle of compounding**. You need to grow your wealth in a tax-FREE account, paying low fees. I will show how to use a special tax haven that can provide a tax-advantaged income source all your life. If you use this account correctly, the **tax-FREE** status is worth over $300,000 extra to you. Taxes are the greatest killer of wealth.

This account, called a "**Wealth Reserve**™" by my colleague, Dan Keppel, grows without taxation as it accumulates. Unlike a regular account, you don't pay taxes every year on the dividends or earnings of your account. When you let your balance compound, you can reach your goal in less time. See page 22. You can do this because you invest in a proven long-term investment—shares of growing companies worldwide.

After you accumulate a sizable balance—say $150,000—you can borrow from it to buy things like appliances and used cars. You pay cash and avoid paying interest to a bank. You can also use it to cover your insurance deductibles and save paying some premium amounts. Of course larger risks are covered by your regular high-deductible policies.

The **miracle of compounding** works best if you use a mutual fund account at the lowest cost you can find. I show you how to set up a low-cost "**Wealth Reserve**™" at no cost. I show you how to pick low-cost investments for long-term growth. You don't need to give up HALF your nest egg to someone who picks your securities. No one can predict the future of any security or fund.

Another benefit of this trust account is that it allows you to make equal contributions monthly. This is called "dollar cost averaging." It is convenient to invest the same amount monthly. If you and your spouse contribute $250 a month, each of you could have $1,000,000 or your family could reach $1 million in less time. By investing a fixed amount each month, you can buy shares at the least cost possible. You buy more shares when the price is low.

If your investing is done automatically, you have a better chance of success. **Automatic investing** makes investing a habit. The habit is actually another step of building wealth. You can't miss making a contribution because you forget about the money coming out of your bank account. The people who succeed at building wealth are those who NEVER stop saving and investing.

Your 401k or 403b works just like a **Wealth Reserve**™ except you *never* have to pay taxes on the accumulations. Most employer-sponsored plans are tax-deferred NOT tax-FREE. The difference can be over $300,000. It is better than an annuity as a legacy for your heirs too. <u>Heirs don't have to pay your income taxes after you're gone</u>.

The **Wealth Reserve**™ may be the best way to accumulate wealth *if* your employer does not match your deposits. However, you can contribute much more to a 401k than a **Wealth Reserve**™ – up to $17,500 (2014) versus $5,500. Both accounts will compound earnings. One will be **tax-FREE** now AND in retirement. The point of both accounts is for contributions to grow without taxes for a number of years. It is best to start with a **Wealth Reserve**™ which has a limit of $5,500. It may provide higher long-term accumulations than a 401k because there are zero, **$0 taxes** ever.

Unlike other methods of investing for the future, a **Wealth Reserve**™ can provide a lifetime of tax-FREE growth. This is a powerful strategy! It uses the most powerful financial force available—**compounding** of high earnings over time. It avoids the greatest **killer** of wealth-building—TAXES. You pay no taxes on the accumulations and no taxes on the withdrawals later. And you don't pay the $3-5,000 broker or advisor fees every year either.

Below are 10 steps to *Earn More*. You invest in high-earning securities over a period of time. You let compounding work its miracle. You pay $250 a month, $99,000 for $1,000,000 over time. You don't stop investing when the market goes up and down. You make investing a habit. That is how compounding happens.

I explain the steps to accumulating $1,000,000:

1. Create a $1,000,000 tax-FREE accumulation.
2. Use a tax-favored lifetime investment account.
3. Compound high earnings.
4. Automate monthly contributions.
5. Use low-cost mutual funds.
6. Buy a large group of stocks of growing companies worldwide.
7. Keep expenses less than income.

8. Buy only the financial services you need.
9. Manage the account only once a year.
10. Take tax-FREE income each year.

Building wealth requires patience. If you are self-employed, you understand that it takes time to build a business. You have to have the right product and then find the customers to serve at a price that enables you to earn a living and profit to expand.

If you work for others, you don't have to be a genius to become financially independent—just be patient. Wealthy people control their spending by various methods. Some have goals and budgets that help them build their spending and investing habits. Some are thrifty. <u>Working millionaires</u> spend less than they make.

Wealthy people have learned that there is no quick way to become wealthy. Accumulating assets requires the investing habit. They learned the habit and saw that the habit paid off over time. They let the miracle of compounding work. They don't pay high taxes or fees. ALL their money compounds and is taxed little.

It does not take a lot of time to manage your account. In fact, it takes only an hour to set up a **Wealth Reserve**™ and takes only 1 hour per year to manage it. As master investor Warren Buffett said:

We continue to make more money when *snoring* than when active.

Building wealth is more about NOT doing something with your investments. Activity in investing usually is the result of fear or greed. Activity usually costs more than the gains.

Wealthy people know about the **miracle of compounding**. Isn't it time we all learn. If we invest $250 per spouse, we may have $1 million in 28 years, $2 million in 33 years. $250 a month is only $9 a day. Pensions, IRAs and annuities are taxable. Your *tax shelter* provides security for life because you have 25-30% more to spend. Your account is FREE of state and federal taxes.

Your choice: **$80,000 or $20,000 a year in retirement income.**

1

$1,000,000 tax-FREE

Building a $1 million tax-FREE account takes time. If we own a business, it would take a lifetime. We would have to find and sell the right product to the right customer in a profitable manner. It is difficult to come up with a completely new product or way to sell it like Apple has done. If we are lucky, we could buyout our boss after working at a skilled trade for years. Many wealthy people have followed this path. They are *The Working Millionaires*.

Another way to build wealth is to take some of our salary from working for others and invest it. We can accumulate $1,000,000 over time, depending on the type of investments we make. Using a high-cost 'managed' account, it takes over 72 years. Using a low-cost tax-FREE fund, it takes about 33 years.

We can understand how this can happen from our experience with a bank savings account and a stock mutual fund. Time is the key to accumulating wealth. Wealthy people have most of their money in company stocks or mutual funds. We can't afford to buy just one company stock—it may fail. Our investment of $250 a month needs to go to a mutual fund with many stocks.

If we are going to accumulate $1,000,000 in about 33 years, we need to find investments that can earn 10% to 12% a year, year after year. We need to understand reward and risk. If we want to have a balance of $1 million, we would have to wait 73 years for our $250 a month to grow in a managed fund. Brokers and advisors charge more because they think they can beat the market all the time. They can't. This is not good for long-term investing.

Investing in low-cost stock mutual funds provides our best chance of success. Historically, the value of a stock market mutual fund—a bunch of stocks—has varied greatly in any one year. However, over time, the value has ALWAYS increased. This is the reason wealthy people have most of their money in the stocks of growing companies.

Remember, we are looking for an investment that compounds our money at 10-12% year after year. The reward and risk profile of owning a bunch of stocks is like owning a business—in any one year, we might have a loss or we might profit. But over time we have more profits than losses and thus succeed.

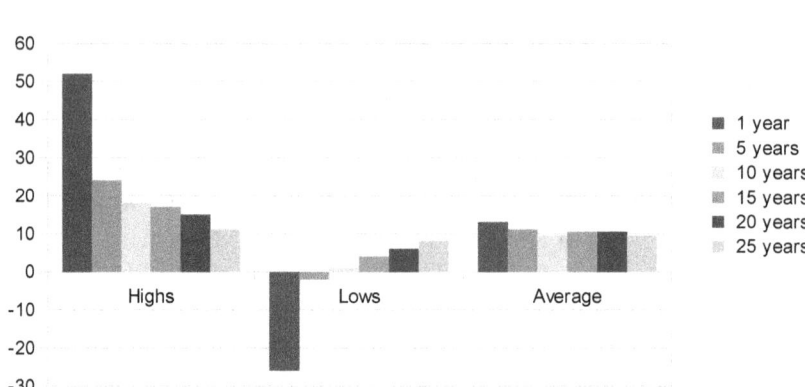

Range of annual returns of stocks, 1950 – 2000

Bank savings are a great place to park our money for a year in case we need it to repair our car, appliances or house. However, bank savings are not really an investment. People who put all their money in the bank because they think it is "safe" are not thinking about the long-term. They are actually losing money. Inflation is eating away at the value of their savings.

Inflation is historically about 3%. If we earn 3% or less on our money, we are losing purchasing power. This means that it costs $0.49 to mail a <u>first class letter</u> instead of 6 cents as it did in 1970. Sending a letter went up at about 5% a year. In order to have enough money to beat inflation in 10 years, we are going to need to invest our LONG-TERM money in an investment earning more than 5%. This goes for all the money we will need to buy everything we will need in the future. Tax-FREE is a bonus.

There are few investments that we can buy that have the same long-term annual returns of stocks of growing companies. The graph below presents the relative growth of different types of investments and inflation. Over long-periods of time, government bonds grow at a rate a little above the rate of inflation. Large company stocks like GE and P&G grow at a higher rate and thus accumulate larger values in our account. Smaller companies grow much faster and make our account even larger over time. However, as the graph shows, the index line can be very jagged on a monthly and even yearly basis. Values do go up over time.

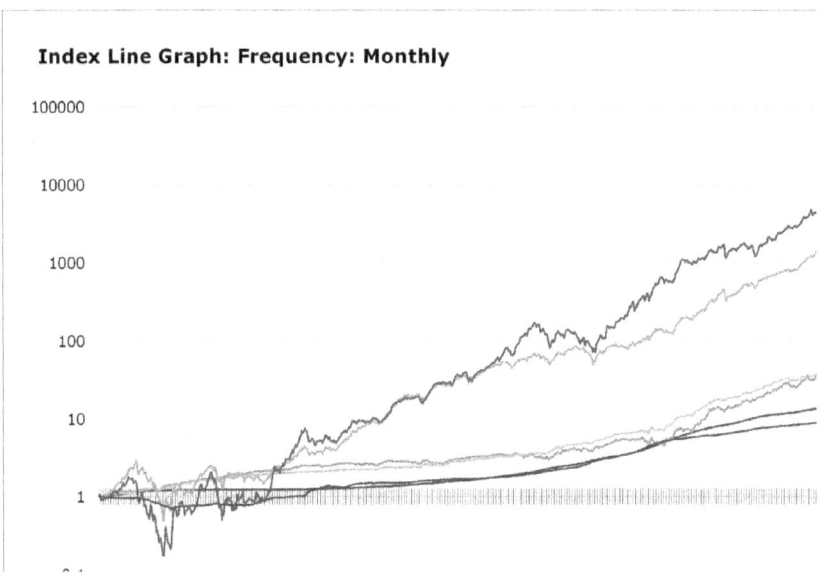

Top line—Small Cap Stocks
2nd line—Large Cap Stocks (S&P 500)
3rd line—US Long-term Corporate Bonds
4th line—Intermediate-term Government Bonds
5th line—US 30 day Government T-bills
6th line—US inflation

Courtesy: Dr. Campbell R. Harvey http://www.duke.edu/~charvey/

This graph makes it pretty clear that in order to accumulate $1,000,000 from monthly contributions, we must buy and hold the securities of growing companies worldwide AND pay **zero** tax on the growth to maximize compounding. We can see clearly that investing in growing company stocks is more likely to get us to our goal in our lifetime than investing in government bonds or a bank savings account.

This graph shows the accumulation over time without paying taxes each year on our earnings or annual fees to an advisor or broker. It does show that over most periods greater than 10 years, our account value grows more with stocks.

Some wealthy people also invest in gold, real estate, and alternative investment schemes. But these investments do NOT usually represent a large portion of their portfolio. These investments do not come without significant costs and significant risk. They do NOT show the same consistent long-term growth pattern that global growing companies do.

According to a number of studies, gold, real estate and other investments have annual average returns under 10%. When we subtract the costs of buying, maintaining and securing these investments, we give up a lot of the gains. We can use an online compounding calculator to become familiar with total values at different rates of return—3, 5, 7, 9, 11, etc.
www.moneychimp.com/calculator/compound_interest_calculator.htm

For instance, if an investment requires taxes to be paid each year, this cancels some of the compounding effect on the total accumulation over time. Since we wish to reach $1 million as soon as possible, we must use a tax-FREE account to hold our investments. Depending on our tax bracket (taxable income) we may reduce our total accumulation by half because we lose the compounding effect. The chart below gives us an idea of what can happen in 30 years. Most pension accounts are tax-DEFERRED not tax-FREE. Taxes have to be paid sometime.

As you have probably guessed, the wealthy have already figured out how to pay less tax on their wealth. The American tax system taxes earned income at higher rates than investment income. Thus we must pay federal and state income taxes, excise taxes, Social Security and Medicare taxes, perhaps unemployment and disability income taxes as well as sales tax on most goods.

For the wealthy, like Warren Buffett, with $65 billions of

assets, most of his income is from <u>investment</u> income—stock gains and dividends. He admitted, "I pay at a lower overall tax rate than all of my office employees." He pays only 17% **total** tax. Listen and weep: http://www.youtube.com/watch?v=Cu5B-2LoC4s.

We are not at that stage yet. Most of us have income which is taxed as earned income and goes straight to the government before we have a chance to pay less tax. Even self-employed people must pay taxes as they go—at least once a quarter.

In order for us to become wealthy we must find a way to avoid paying tax on our $1,000,000 account as it accumulates. Traditional pensions, 401k and IRAs just delay taxes—taxes must be paid later as the money comes out of the account AND at higher earned income tax rates. Thus even when our investment money is growing it is <u>converted to earned</u> income money for tax purposes. Unlike Mr Buffett, we NEVER get to pay the wealthy people (capital gains) rate of 15% total tax.

Luckily, there is now a solution for us to match the tax advantage that the wealthy. In fact, only we can use it. We use a tax-FREE trust to compound the high returns of the stocks of growing companies over time. We avoid the greatest killer of wealth—taxes—and let time transform our $99,000 in contributions into $1 million. Patience and steady investing make our strategy beat the industry myth of genius stock pickers.

It is your choice: **11.11% or 3.69%** and 0% tax on your investment income.

Various investment accumulations

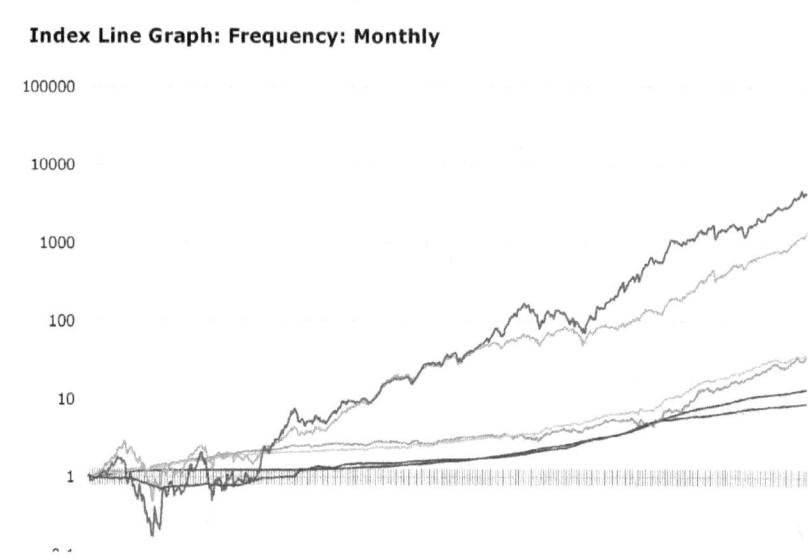

Top line—Small Cap Stocks
2nd line—Large Cap Stocks (S&P 500)
3rd line—US Long-term Corporate Bonds
4th line—Intermediate-term Government Bonds
5th line—US 30 day Government T-bills
6th line—US inflation

Courtesy: Dr. Campbell R. Harvey http://www.duke.edu/~charvey/

2

One account

Create retirement income that is FREE of income tax—add $300,000—using a special IRS account.

The solution to our problem came in 1997. Senator Roth, Rep. DE, introduced the Roth IRA. This tax-FREE account we call a **Wealth Reserve**™ provides the protection we need to allow our contributions to compound without taxation every year AND later when we take them out, we never have to pay taxes on the earnings, dividends and interest we earn on our money. We don't even pay the tax-advantaged rate of the wealthy!

Ben Franklin was wrong! Only death is certain, not taxes. The only thing we give up with this account is an immediate tax deduction. However, compare the value of paying a little more tax now with paying ZERO tax later. We can spend about $30,000 tax-FREE for every $3,000 a year we contributed over time. We can see the fantastic advantage we now have. This is a better deal than most wealthy people have.

Tax-FREE accumulation and tax-FREE income after age 59.5 is a huge bonus. It is like receiving $300,000 FREE on our $1 million account. Also, because we already paid tax on the contributions, we pay no tax if we take the money out for emergencies. This can make a big impact on our borrowing costs when we take money out to buy an appliance, a car, a down payment or disability income.

Using this account, our total contributions of $99,000 over time grow to over $1,000,000 and we don't have to pay any federal or state income tax on the earnings. WOW! Since we pay no tax, Uncle Sam is really helping us meet our goal. All we have to do is use this special IRS tax haven and keep making contributions.

This special account is the IRS §408 trust we call our **"Wealth Reserve**™**"**. We have to follow the rules to gain this amazing tax advantage but the Roth IRA rules are pretty simple—

taxed money goes in and tax-FREE earnings come out after age 59 ½. We can take our contributions out anytime.

Why is this account special? Every other type of investment account requires that taxes be paid now or later. Mutual funds declare gains each year just like a bank CD and we need to pay tax. Our retirement accounts and annuities are tax-deferred. We pay tax when we take money out. Even life insurance with cash value requires taxes to be paid unless it is a death benefit to heirs. Even assets like individual stocks or ETFs or our own company equity held for long term gains will require taxes eventually when sold. The gains in a **Wealth Reserve**™ are FREE—no tax ever.

Contributions are limited to $5,500 (2014), but may rise in future years. http://www.irs.gov/publications/p590/ch02.html There are income limits but most people don't hit the earnings limit of $129,000 (2014) until later. If we are married, the limit is $191,000 (2014). We make our deposit to our **Wealth Reserve**™ automatic so we can't forget or try to time the market.

We may also invest in our employer's Roth 401k if it is offered. The contributions grow tax FREE forever. We can contribute up to $17,500 (2014). We will have tax-FREE income from the account later.

We can make contributions to our Roth 401k only if our employer offers it in the retirement plan. Many young people prefer to be taxed at the beginning of their careers since their salaries do not draw high tax rates yet. The contribution limit may be raised in the future.

There are no limits on an employee's income in determining if he or she can make designated Roth 401(k) contributions. If we decide to invest $10,000 a year for 35 years in a low-cost stock fund inside our employer's Roth 401k plan, we could accumulate $2 million with NO income taxation to pay on the earnings. The tax savings might be worth an extra 30% since our federal and state tax payments are avoided.

The catch: If we take the *earnings* out before age 59.5, we must pay tax and penalty, unless we use $10,000 for our first home, are disabled, or die. The account must be open at least 5 years to take money out. However, if we take out ***contributions***, we pay no tax or penalty. If we pay our 'loan' back to our own account, we can still reach our goal. The hard part is leaving our money alone to grow tax-FREE.

Let's say we need $15,000 to buy a new used car. As we can see from the chart on page 22, taking $15,000 from an account worth $250,000 is very different from taking $15,000 from one worth only $25,000. Both are contributions and are not taxable but borrowing 60% of the account this early stunts its growth.

Our working millionaire would find a way to save the $15,000 separately or keep driving the old car. The power of compounding is too valuable to lose by raiding the account too early. One story about billionaire Buffett will illustrate the habits of the wealthy. Mr Buffett is said to have driven (no chauffeur) his VW Beetle long after he became a multimillionaire. Buffett did not like to lose money and a new car loses 40% of its value quickly. He thought that the $40,000 a new car cost, invested at 12%, is worth about $100,000 in 10 years. So he kept driving the old VW.

Monthly Accumulation at 12% per year										
	5	10	15	20	25	30	35	40	45	50
$100	$8,167	$23,004	$49,958	$98,925	$187,884	$349,496	$643,095	$1,176,477	$2,145,469	$3,905,834
$200	$16,334	$46,008	$99,916	$197,850	$375,768	$698,992	$1,286,190	$2,352,954	$4,290,938	$7,811,668
$300	$24,501	$69,012	$149,874	$296,775	$563,652	$1,048,488	$1,929,285	$3,529,431	$6,436,408	$11,717,502
$500	$40,835	$115,020	$249,790	$494,625	$939,420	$1,747,480	$3,215,475	$5,882,385	$10,727,346	$19,529,169

Most clients are not that frugal. They use their contributions to buy a used car to avoid new car depreciation and new appliances, vacations, and other necessities AFTER they have a sizable account. When both family wage earners contribute to their Roth IRAs, they can easily reach a quarter of a million dollars in 15 years. That means $90,000 are contributions and then some of it can be used to pay cash instead of buying on credit.

Wealthy people use their wealth to pay cash because then they never PAY interest. Paying interest on a debt is the reverse of compounding. Someone else is becoming wealthy from us. The wealthy always EARN interest. They use the chart above or the http://www.moneychimp.com/calculator/compound_interest_calculator.htm to determine what the real cost of buying something on credit will be just like Buffett did. Why give up $80,000 when we can drive the old car a little longer. Buffett could have bought 100 new cars and it wouldn't have changed his wealth or lifestyle, but he didn't. His habit is to live frugally and not look wealthy.

We can use this account (its contributions) to cover our liability insurance deductibles also. We can save thousands of dollars over time by using the highest deductibles on our car, home and health insurance. Self-insurance is also the way to avoid any changes in our policy costs. Insurers are less likely to drop us if we don't make claims for small amounts. If we take care of our out-of-pocket medical expenses, we may find a low-cost comprehensive policy if we need to buy health coverage.

The rules for the use of our "**Wealth Reserve**™" account are manageable by ourselves. We don't need an advisor. They are found at irs.gov/retirement/article/0,,id=137307,00.html. Our account trustee can answer most questions. We don't need to pay an attorney. All of the large low-cost mutual funds firms are trustees. We will discuss the best firms available below.

We can start this account with most of the firms with no upfront charges. Most do charge an annual fee for the investments and an annual bookkeeping fee. We will consider the specific investment options later. We will use low-cost firms.

It is important to pick a trustee with the least costs since over time the annual costs can really destroy our accumulations. For instance, if we use a brokerage firm as trustee, we might have to pay 2% or more each year on the balance. The difference is huge. If both spouses have a low-cost account with contributions of $250 a month for 33 years, they could accumulate $2,000,000. If they use a high-cost broker/advisor, both accounts may hit only $800,000. Depending on earnings of 8-10% using a broker or advisor (fees of 2% per year), they could really hurt themselves. We need to watch the costs. We will compare firms below.

We can open our account at any age as long as we have *earned* income. Stock dividends or interest do not count. Any job will do. We don't even need a job requiring a W-2 to prove it. A part-time, weekend or night job will do. Any cash-only work will also qualify. Accountants recommend that receipts and records be maintained. We could even work for ourselves in a home-office business.

Nontaxable distributions from a Roth IRA won't affect our eligibility for student aid either. Later, in retirement, this money won't affect our social security benefits as of the rules today.

We can make contributions to both our individual Roth IRA and our Roth account at work (401k, 403b, 457b). The limits change each year, so check Pub 590: http://www.irs.gov/pub/irs-pdf/p590.pdf. The 2014 limits are $5,500 ($1,000) and $17,500

($5,500) respectively. (If we are age 50 or older, we can make a catch-up contribution to both.)

Avoiding taxes on our annual gains supercharges our accumulations. This special account is the IRS §408 trust we call a "**Wealth Reserve**™". We have to follow the rules of a Roth IRA to gain this amazing tax advantage. The rules are pretty simple: pay smaller tax on contributions now in exchange for NO tax on huge gains later. We can use the contributions to avoid paying interest to banks for our major purchases. We earn interest, we don't pay interest.

The **Wealth Reserve**™ is the perfect tax shelter for working people. And it is free to set up and run each year. In the future, we can spend tax-FREE $30,000 for every $3,000 we invest today.

It's your choice: **spend $80,000 or $20,000.**

Client Tom's account, investing $3,000 per year, 1962-2003

Return	Balance
24%	3,720
16%	7,795
12%	12,091
-10%	13,582
24%	20,561
11%	26,153
-8%	26,821
4%	31,013
14%	38,775
19%	49,713
-14%	45,333
-26%	35,766
37%	53,110
24%	69,576
-8%	66,770
6%	73,956
18%	90,809
32%	123,827
-5%	120,486
22%	150,653
21%	185,920
6%	200,255
32%	268,297
19%	322,843
5%	342,135
17%	403,808
32%	536,987
-3%	523,787
31%	690,091
8%	748,538
10%	826,692
2%	846,286
38%	1,172,015
23%	1,445,268
33%	1,926,197
28%	2,469,372
21%	2,991,570
-9%	2,725,059
-12%	2,403,420
-22%	1,874,601
29%	2,412,905

3

Compound high earnings

Compounding our high investment earnings is key to creating enough retirement income. The rich get richer—the top 1% take 23.5% of all income (up from 8.9%). And, as many millionaires have said, "the first million is the hardest." If we start with $3,000, it will take us about 33 years of investing $3,000 a year in stock funds to reach $1,000,000. (And only in a tax-FREE account.) However, when we reach half a million, we only have to double our money to reach $1 million. Investors in stock funds, earning 10-12% on average, do this in 7 years without adding new money. Our tax-FREE account makes it easier to reach our goal.

Compounding of high earnings means that we make money on our last period's accumulations. The progression looks like the Tom's account values on the previous page. Notice that our balance can double in a couple of good years. This happens because we are not just adding $3,000 per year, but adding up to 38% of the previous year's accumulation to our balance. We are making money on top of our money with no extra effort on our part. During this 40 year period, his balance fell some years. In fact, it fell 14% and then gained 26%, but then rose 37% and 24%.

Wealthy people don't panic. They have learned that compounding over the long-term is the only way they can build wealth. There are no successful get-rich-quick schemes. To reach their goal, they know there will be setbacks on paper. No business grows steadily upward all the time. They have seen the losses before and they don't sell their assets in a panic.

We will buy assets that "grow by themselves." We will have security because our ***purchasing power*** will grow over time. If we doubt that the wealthy invest in the stock market for security, take a look at the long-term returns for various Vanguard mutual funds where they put their money. These funds have provided investors with $ millions for their retirement. During the recent recession, Vanguard had inflows not outflows.

The wealthy earn 10% to 12% on their money. We could buy

all ten Vanguard funds and receive 11% total return with less risk than owning just one fund. When one fund is down, others are up.

2013 Total Return	Fund	Long-term Return*	Longevity
32.3%	500 Index	11.0%*	since 1976
18.4%	Energy	13.2%	since 1984
38.4%	Extended Market Idx	11.2%	since 1987
43.2%	Health	17.1%	since 1984
23.0%	International Growth	11.2%	since 1981
39.7%	PRIMECAP	13.7%	since 1984
37.6%	Small Cap Index	10.9%	since 1960
9.2%	Wellesley Income	10.1%	since 1970
36.1%	Windsor	11.6%	since 1958
30.7%	Windsor II	11.1%	since 1985
30.9%	Average	12.1%	

*Average Annual Returns as of 12/31/13.

This kind of security comes from our regular contributions ... and patience. The miracle of compounding only works its magic on our **Wealth Reserve**™ when we give it TIME. The wealthy give their money time to compound. We must keep our money working and avoid tax and fees every year on the gains. We must maintain our contribution schedule because each $250 added is worth $2,500 to us later. We use the compound interest calculator so we know the future value of our account:
moneychimp.com/calculator/compound_interest_calculator.htm.

Compounding of high earnings requires patience but has a big bang. Most people who become wealthy see years of spurts of growth and loss in their account. At the beginning of the accumulation, especially if we have a loss or two, we are very tempted to quit making contributions. The account just doesn't seem to adding up to an inspiring total.

It took client Tom 21 years to get to $150,000. Then it only took 14 years to get to a $1,172,015. After only 4 years, it became $3,000,000. Shortly thereafter he "lost" over a million dollars!

This client stuck with it and was successful in reaching his goal but there are many who did not. Most people who are not wealthy already, have a hard time believing it can happen with their patience. They just don't have the experience of how compounding works to keep faith in its outcome eventually.

If you already have a **Wealth Reserve**℠ with significant values, you can use it to do your gift and estate planning. You don't have to take the money out beginning at age 70½, unlike the regular IRA or pension. You can let it grow. You can name your family members as beneficiaries which will be effective for both property law and income tax purposes. Obviously, as beneficiary, your grandchild could just liquidate the account and thus lose the value for their "Gift of a Lifetime." Wealthy people use a knowledgable attorney to make sure their wealth passes to those who make the most of it.

Once an account becomes sizable, we don't need to add contributions to it. Usually, by the time we stop regular employment, we aren't making contributions. This account cannot accept contributions unless they are the result of earned income. Some wealthy people continue to work after age 65 because they love what they do and want to continue. Obviously, they don't need to work. The miracle of compounding continues.

One of the best examples of the potential of growth by compounding is seen in the accumulation of investor Anne Scheiber. With below average wages, this woman invested in quality companies which paid dividends and gains. She reinvested her dividends and gains and at her death gave $22 million to Yeshiva University for a scholarship designed to help support deserving women.

Getting "the first million is the hardest." Since we don't make millions from employment, compounding high earnings is the only way we are going to reach our goal in our lifetime. Compounding works because we leverage TIME in our favor— Time instead of money.

We use only low-cost mutual funds in a TAX-FREE account so we earn 10-12% over time instead of paying HALF in taxes and fees. We earn more and create greater retirement income.

The annual returns of growing companies

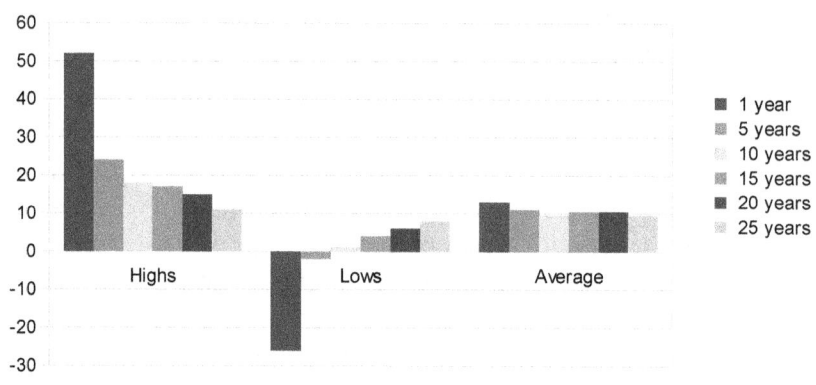

Range of annual returns of stocks, 1950 – 2000

4

Automate contributions

One of the techniques for building wealth is to maintain consistent contributions to our **Wealth Reserve**™. This helps take our emotions out of the process of building wealth. If we do not watch the stock market or our account balance regularly, we will be less likely to panic. If we don't have to write and send the check each month, we don't think about how our account is doing.

Our normal reaction to having money in an account is to watch it, guard it, think about how it is doing, compare its size and rate of growth. All of these actions are fine for stock TRADERS. But we are silent partners in growing companies. We believe that global businesses will continue to grow. However, most people don't look at their wealth building in that way. Most people do not think of this account as a stake in many growing businesses. They see investing in stocks as playing bingo at the casino.

One way we can help change our thinking is to try to put the account out of our immediate concern by making the contributions automatic. Like the Social Security contributions we make every payday, the contributions come out of our pay automatically. This can happen easily with a Roth 401k since our Plan administrator will deduct the amount we specify at Plan enrollment. In the same manner, we can have the Roth IRA trustee debit our checking account automatically every period.

As one client told me, "I never see the deduction, so I never miss it." Of course this client has already identified the $250 he has committed to his $1,000,000 future. He says that he was wasting $250 on fees and extra insurance. He had been doing that for years because he never took the trouble to set his goals for short-term and long-term timelines. He took my advice and went through his spending on financial services. He used our *Guides* to find the $250 a month he was wasting on products and services he would never use or need. In Dan Keppel's amazon.com/Insiders-Guides-Discount-Financial-Services/ you will find "tricks of the trade" that we insiders use to buy directly from quality manufacturers.

Many people have trouble keeping up the habit of investing every month. Some emergency always interupts this process. The delay in the periodic contributions causes the compounding effect to be reduced. The interruption is like starting the investment process late. This chart shows us what starting early or not putting off the investments can do. Over time, the delay compounds the lack of accumulation. Starting 5 years later means ending up with HALF the amount we were shooting for. It is hard to believe that missing that $250 a month for 5 years or $15,000 can reduce our total from $600,000 to $300,000. It's easy to say **I will start later**.

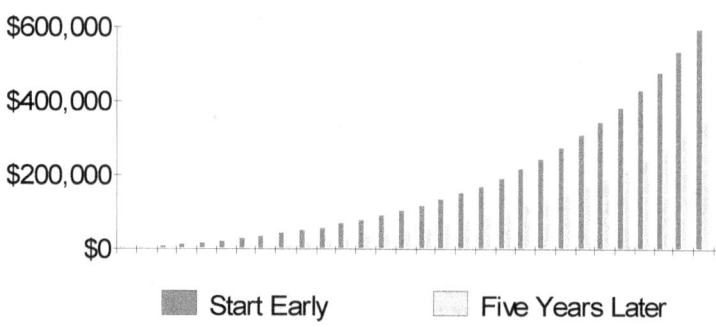

This is why our contributions to the account should not pass through our hands. We should have the money taken directly from our bank account by the trustee. Contributions are after-tax so you can take them, if necessary, with no tax payable. Nontaxable distributions from a Roth IRA won't affect your eligibility for student aid either. Later, in retirement, this money won't affect your Social Security benefits as of the rules today.

The second reason why this technique for developing wealth works is that when contributions are automatic, we do not have the temptation to try to time the market. Many people want to know the secret to timing the market so that they can invest right at the bottom of market cycles and sell at the peak of the market.

Unfortunately, it is a myth that we can do this all the time. Again, this is our misconception of how building wealth works.

Yes, there are lucky gamblers. However, they are the exception. We are trying to build wealth over time. We want to end up with $1,000,000 tax-FREE. We are silent partners in building businesses that produce dividends and gains over time. We are not placing our contributions on red or black at the casino.

Our account grows with steady contributions because in the month we buy $250 of company stocks in a mutual fund, we receive less shares when the price is high and more shares when the price is low. Studies have shown that this is better than trying to find the market lows. It is not possible to know when the shares we buy will be at their lowest cost in the year going forward. Again, over time, we will own more shares at the least cost because we are buying more when the price is low.

This can be illustrated by considering how hard it is to find the lowest price at any given time in the market. There were ONLY 40 days from 1950 to 2007 that produced 70% of all the S&P 500 index's total returns. That is 40 out of 14,528. We can't possibly know when to buy into the businesses represented in the mutual fund we are using. We will lose money if we try to become traders who time the market. See John Bogle's analysis in *Don't Count on It*, p 169.

The key to building wealth is steady growth. We have seen that over time, stocks of growing companies have the most consistent record of providing 10-12% annual returns. We just don't know which companies and which time to invest are best. Luckily, we don't have to know. We need to understand the bigger picture—next page.

The bigger picture is that we want our account accumulation to grow exponentially. We want to take advantage of the **miracle of compounding**. Since we don't have a million dollars, we are going to have to be patient to acquire it. We want every dollar we invest to count. We have $250 a month to invest so we have to rely on consistent buying of shares to reach our goal.

Accumulations double in value every 7-10 years if they are concentrated in the top two lines below. Of course the stock market doesn't move up at 10-12% EACH year. However, our wealth account will double and double and double so that by age 65, we could have over $1 million. Notice how the account values in the chart on page 22 for our client move from $1 million to $2 million in 8 years, even with 3 years of losses. Of course, a million dollars will be worth less in the future because of inflation. But we will certainly appreciate our account values later no matter what our contributions are now. Consistency builds wealth.

Cumulative Wealth

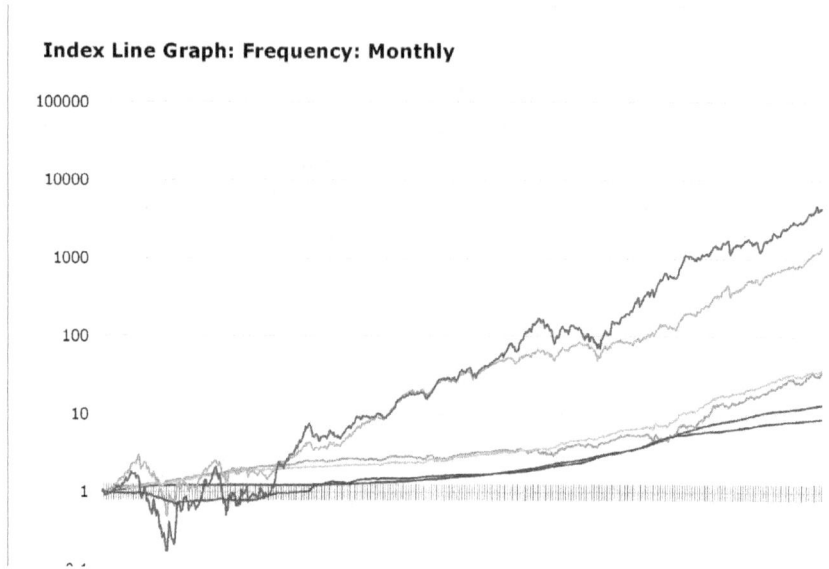

Top line—Small Cap Stocks
2nd line—Large Cap Stocks (S&P 500)
3rd line—US Long-term Corporate Bonds
4th line—Intermediate-term Government Bonds
5th line—US 30 day Government T-bills
6th line—US inflation

Courtesy: Dr. Campbell R. Harvey http://www.duke.edu/~charvey/

And the bonus of this geometric account growth is that it does not quit even after we stop adding our monthly contributions. Once the account has reached a certain mass, let's say after 20 years of contributions or $60,000, it will keep compounding. On page 32 we show you how this worked for contributions of $2,000 to a virtual account invested in the U.S. stock market (500 Index) over time.

We can see in the chart "Cumulative Wealth" above that over time, wealth accumulates at different rates depending on the type of assets we buy. For anyone who invested in smaller companies over any given 15 year period, the benefits were outstanding. For ***each $1,000*** invested in 1940, $3,000,000 was the total return by the 1990's. Investing more cautiously in the large companies of the S&P 500, for instance, our $1,000 would have grown to almost a $1,000,00 by 2000. Yes, the lines are not perfectly straight, but growing $250 a month to $1,000,000 is definitely worth the ups and downs. Inflation is designated by the bottom line here. Putting all our money in a bank CD would accumulate at a rate represented by a line near that bottom line.

Of course, these different rates of wealth accumulation assume two important factors—NO taxes and LOW costs. We have eliminated the first killer of wealth—TAXES—by using a tax-FREE trust account. Costs of the investment type we use can also kill your total accumulations. My whole industry is built on the extraction of these costs from the accounts of investors. We must use low-cost stock funds or we may give up 63% of our account.

One of the most difficult parts of building wealth is sticking with the program. If we put our monthly contributions on automatic, we will have no interruptions. If we instruct our trustee to debit our savings or checking account every month, we have a high probability of meeting our goals over time.

Create $80,000 retirement income by putting investing on automatic deduction like a utility bill. We forget we are investing in our future and thus we actually create it.

$2,000 Annual Stock Market Investment 1950- '70- '80- '90- 2013

Year	Returns	Balance	Balance	Balance	Balance
		$2,000			
1950	31%	$2,620			
1951	24%	$5,729			
1952	18%	$9,120			
1953	-1%	$11,009			
1954	52%	$19,773			
1955	31%	$28,523			
1956	5%	$32,049			
1957	-11%	$30,304			
1958	43%	$46,194			
1959	12%	$53,978			
1960	1%	$56,538			
1961	26%	$73,757			
1962	-8%	$69,697			
1963	24%	$88,904			
1964	16%	$105,449			
1965	12%	$120,342			
1966	-10%	$110,108			
1967	24%	$139,014			
1968	11%	$156,526			
1969	-8%	$145,844	2,000		
1970	4%	$153,757	2,080		
1971	14%	$177,563	4,651		
1972	19%	$213,681	7,915		
1973	-14%	$185,485	8,527		
1974	-26%	$138,739	7,790		
1975	37%	$192,813	13,412		
1976	24%	$241,568	19,111		
1977	-8%	$224,082	19,422		
1978	6%	$239,647	22,707		
1979	18%	$285,144	29,155	2,000	
1980	32%	$379,030	41,124	2,640	
1981	-5%	$361,978	40,968	4,408	
1982	22%	$444,053	52,421	7,818	
1983	21%	$539,724	65,850	11,879	
1984	6%	$574,228	71,921	14,712	
1985	32%	$760,621	97,575	22,060	
1986	19%	$907,519	118,494	28,632	
1987	5%	$954,995	126,519	32,163	
1988	17%	$1,119,684	150,367	39,971	
1989	32%	$1,480,623	201,125	55,402	2,000
1990	-3%	$1,438,144	197,031	55,680	1,940
1991	31%	$1,886,589	260,731	75,560	5,161
1992	8%	$2,039,676	283,749	83,765	7,734
1993	10%	$2,245,843	314,324	94,342	10,708
1994	2%	$2,292,800	322,651	98,268	12,962
1995	38%	$3,166,824	448,018	138,370	20,647
1996	23%	$3,897,654	553,522	172,656	27,856
1997	33%	$5,186,540	738,844	232,292	39,709
1998	28%	$6,641,331	948,281	299,894	53,387
1999	21%	$8,038,430	1,149,839	365,291	67,019
2000	-9%	$7,316,791	1,048,174	334,235	62,807
2001	-12%	$6,447,855	925,203	296,223	57,095
2002	-22%	$5,024,437	722,291	232,316	46,035
2003	29%	$6,459,474	930,787	301,119	61,730
2004	11%	$7,164,483	1,034,274	336,099	70,664
2005	5%	$7,512,677	1,084,540	352,433	74,098
2006	15%	$8,694,884	1,259,259	412,409	90,450
2007	5%	$9,163,538	1,327,133	434,638	95,325
2008	-39%	$5,601,431	813,388	268,074	60,754
2009	27%	$7,116,358	952,155	342,993	79,699
2010	15%	$8,186,112	1,097,278	396,742	93,954
2011	2%	$8,347,378	1,118,894	404,558	95,805
2012	16%	$9,666,264	1,295,679	468,478	110,942
2013	32%	$12,759,468	1,710,296	618,390	146,443
Avg.	12%	12%	11%	13%	11%

I.A.N. LLC © 2014   1/2/14   TheInsidersGuides.com

Ibbotson Associates **Stocks average 11.4% per year, bonds 5%, CDs 3%.** Stocks have gone up as much as 54% and as low as –43% in 1 year, up to 28% or down to –12% in 5 years, up 20% or down 0% in 10 years, up 18% or up 3% in 20 years. Short term bonds have gone up 14% or up 0% in 1 year, up 11% or up 0% in 5 years, up 9% or up 0% in 10 years, up 10% or up 1% in 20 years. Check returns for any period: http://www.moneychimp.com/features/market_cagr.htm

5

Low-cost mutual funds

"In every single time period and data point tested, low-cost funds beat high-cost funds."

According to an unbiased Morningstar study, low-cost funds beat high-cost funds, PERIOD. However, the myth of Wall Street is that you must pay more for good performance. Not true. We all know that for most goods, paying more (for packaging and TV commercials) does not guarantee a better product.

The **best predictor** of your investing and wealth building success is **low cost**. It is common sense that there are just too many variables in the success of growing companies' stocks for anyone to be able to pick them in advance on a consistent basis. A low-cost stock mutual fund provides the best chance of maximizing our accumulations as the market leaders change over time.

Contrary to Wall Street's hype, it does not matter which stocks are rising or falling at any given time. If our account holds a broad representation of stocks and our investment costs are low, we will benefit over the long haul. We own them all, at cost!

Since the annual returns of stock funds have averaged 10-12% over time, we want to pick the lowest cost mutual funds available. A stock fund that reflects the overall market is called an index fund. This kind of fund costs only 0.05% ($5 per $10,000). Our account will compound at or near the 10-12% over time since the costs are low compared to ones that charge 1.5-3%. If we use the high-cost stock funds in our account, we will earn about 8% over time. These funds pay managers high salaries with expensive bonuses. The fund owners and sales staff are paid well also. Mutual funds are the cash cow of Wall Street—NO REFUNDS.

The chart below makes it clear. Over time, the costs we pay each year will cut our total accumulation by a THIRD or more. Instead of compounding at 10-12% annually on average, some people give up 1.5-3% of the earnings on their money to the middle person. They end up with less.

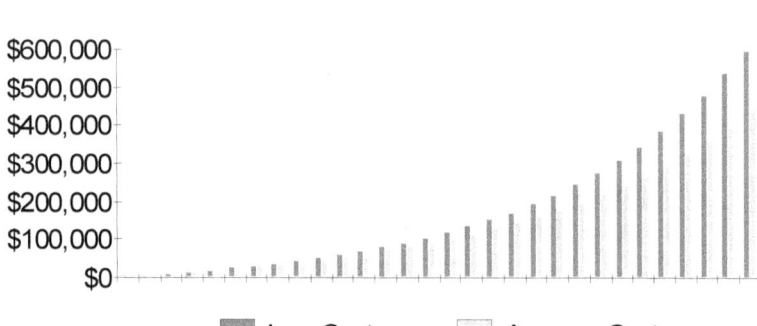

Wall Street says that we can earn more by paying a star manager to pick the right stocks on an ongoing basis. The money "experts" say we get what we pay for and a proven stock-picking manager will overcome the extra costs and make more for us.

The problem is that this myth has been proven wrong. The lowest cost funds don't pay a star manager and owner big bucks but come out ahead over time. There are simply too many variables for anyone or computer program to pick the winning stocks all the time. Some of the lowest cost funds are called index funds. When we buy an index, we are buying a piece of many companies that reflect the market. This gives us the same annual returns as the overall market over time. We pay tiny expenses.

Many studies have proven that index funds beat funds run by stock pickers over time. Low-cost index funds beat 86% of funds with a stock-picking manager. *BusinessWeek* Apr 2009. http://www.businessweek.com/investing/insights/blog/archives/2009/04/where_have_all.html.

When we investigate the experiences of the best money managers in the world, we find they recommend index funds to most people who invest as silent partners. Here are their statements:

Warren Buffett is probably history's greatest investor, in terms of results with $60 BILLION ($60 thousand million dollars) so far. He buys *companies* that provide valuable services to a great number of people. His company owns parts of Coke, GEICO, Fruit of the Loom, Benjamin Moore, BNSF RR, Acme Brick, Heinz, etc. berkshirehathaway.com/

He told Reuters: "<u>A very low-cost index is going to beat a majority of the amateur-managed money or professionally-managed money</u>."

Compare the odds of selecting the correct mutual fund. A fund's chance of beating the market in EACH year is 3 out of 100. nytimes.com/2009/02/22/your-money/stocks-and-bonds/22stra.html

<u>Peter Lynch</u>, brilliant manager, Magellan Fund "…you'd be just as well off if you'd invested in the <u>S&P 500</u>." *One Up on Wall Street*, 1989, p. 240.

<u>Jonathan Clements</u>, formerly ***The Wall Street Journal***
"Most people can do it themselves. ... By indexing, you don't just ensure that you will do better than most other investors. You will also enjoy the advantage of 'relative certainty.' . . . For most investors, Vanguard will be the place to go." *You've Lost It, Now What? How to beat the bear market and still retire on time*, 2003, p. 62, 70.

<u>Charles D. Ellis</u>, money managers' consultant
"The premise . . . that professional investment managers *can* beat the market . . . appears to be false. It is a loser's game. ... clients would have done better in a market fund." Returns are "splendidly predictable—on average and over time." *Investment Policy, How to Win the Loser's Game*, 1985, p. 5, 20, 34.

<u>Jane Bryant Quinn</u>, consumer advisor
"I'm a longtime booster of <u>index mutual funds</u>. These funds follow the market as a whole. Tons of research has shown that most money managers don't beat the markets they invest in, after costs. Maybe your own stocks or funds have excelled in the past couple of years. But in most cases, you've also been taking extra risk. The odds of superior performance are against you, in the long run. Indexing puts the odds on your side." *Los Angeles Business Journal*, May 8, 2000

Charles Schwab founder, discount broker
"I put my money where my mouth is: most of the mutual fund investments I have are in index funds, approximately 75%. My core investments are index funds. Experienced investors have discovered that in any given year, on average, only 20 to 30 percent of mutual funds outperform the market. That is why I recommend index funds…"
Mr. Schwab tells of one of his friends who owned many well-run funds. After keeping track of all the dividends, taxes, reinvestments tax basis and statements, he found he earned the same return as the index of these funds. After selling them all, he bought the index fund. He has "what he wanted in the first place: diversification, tax advantages, one statement, and lower expenses." *Guide to Financial Independence*, 1998, pp. 90, 103, 111.

Motley Fool, Internet site about investing
"Almost ***everything*** that you will ever read about mutual funds beyond, "Buy an index fund." is superfluous to your long-term success in investing in mutual funds." Fool.com.

Walter Updegrave, senior editor, *Money*
"Mutual fund picking would be easier if there was one you could count on to outperform 70% or so of its competitors over long stretches of a decade or more. It's called an index fund. Although less than 10% of investors own an index fund, they are "one of the best-kept secrets" on Wall Street. My unabashed aim is to convince you to put at least a part of your money into one or more of these funds. You have a far less than a 50% chance of beating the market…. I strongly recommend that you make index funds your primary holding…." *The Right Way to Invest in Mutual Funds*, 1996, p 189-194.

Andrew Tobias, financial writer
"Scrimp and save, putting whatever you can into no-load, low-expense stock market index funds, both U.S. and foreign. You will do better than 80% of your friends and neighbors." *My Vast Fortune*, 1997, p. 158.
There are many books written on the subject of index and "managed" funds. If you wish to vanquish the hype and understand

investing, skim *A Random Walk Down Wall Street* by Princeton University's Burton Malkiel. Here are the reasons why smart insiders use low-cost funds:

1. Both stock and bond index funds provide better returns than 86% of managed funds for periods greater than 10 years.
2. You earn more because you pay lower costs and taxes.
3. Low-cost funds build greater wealth over time.
4. Low-cost funds can be less volatile because they reflect whole sectors of the market.
5. Low-cost funds offer better diversification.
6. You know what you are paying for. No high-salary managers.
7. Low-cost funds don't require you to hope the manager will predict the future correctly. The odds of doing it are 1 in 15,000 each year separately. Over time, all funds provide average returns minus their costs.
8. Low-cost funds are easy to buy.

> "Professional money management is a gigantic rip-off."
> Bill Gross, star bond manager, *Everything You've Heard About Investing is Wrong*

Summary of many studies about index investing

First, fund managers try to predict the future of the market when they buy and sell securities in their funds. There is no proof this can be done well over time. Yesterday's winners are usually tomorrow's losers. The AVERAGE market return has been 10-12%, so a few managers will beat the average by luck—Just not the same ones every year. nytimes.com/2008/07/13/business/13stra.html
Second, the costs of the manager, their staff and operations must be paid for by you whether or not they earn you a dime. It is always better to pay as little as possible for the same performance. Costs can take 63% of your returns over time. Surprisingly, while the stock index rose 11%, investors with high paid managers averaged only **3.69%** annually for 30 years to 2013 (QAIB). DALBARinc.
Third, high cost managers get paid for increasing the size of their funds, not for making you rich. Bringing in more money is a full-

time job. It is expensive to market the funds given that there are now thousands available. It is inevitable that popular funds will grow until they produce average returns with high expenses. <u>Managers want to be rich</u>, not right.

Fourth, there is much less chance of you being treated poorly by fund management if the structure and governance are <u>customer-oriented</u> like Vanguard's and TIAA-CREF's are.

Fifth, many professional managers and Wall Street insiders place their core assets in low-cost index funds.

The best predictor of the success of a mutual fund is its cost. Usually the least expensive funds that match market averages beat the more expensive managed funds. Low-cost market index funds buy all the securities represented in a broad market. The goal of an index fund is to match its market. Low-cost index funds have provided returns that beat 80-90% of managed funds over the long-term. No manager has been able to predict the future so the returns regress to the mean.

The numbers do NOT support the Wall Street myths. We earn more when we pay less for the same market growth. The smart money is on the averages not the long shot, unless we have <u>insider information</u>.

"In every single time period and data point tested, low-cost funds beat high-cost funds."

6

Global growth

If we want to have a $1,000,000 tax-FREE account and produce $80,000 income, we need a way to make it happen—a strategy. To be able to have a nest egg of $1 million requires that we know how and where to invest, invest regularly, invest properly, monitor accumulations along the way, and get help when we need it. We need a clear plan that takes only one hour to set up and only one hour per year to manage. Complicated plans just don't work for most people. Complicated strategies cost more to execute.

Picking *individual* stocks as a strategy is not likely to work for us. Professional managers and day traders have had limited success **over time**. Our strategy is to build wealth as a silent partner in growing global companies. Since it is unlikely that we (or anyone else) will be able to pick the next Google or Apple, we invest in a large group of firms. We do not need to fear picking the wrong one or picking one at the wrong time. As the founder of the largest mutual fund firm, John Bogle, says: "Don't look for the needle. Buy the haystack."

This is contrary to the myth of Wall Street 'professionals.' They make their living claiming to find the needle every year and we pay the price—3.69% not 11.11%. Professionals promise that they can find the next big one and we pay them well because we want to be rich. They take the difference to the bank. For example, Bill Gross earned $2.3 billion managing a fund that is failing.

Like the lottery, we kid ourselves into thinking that "someone has to win, why not me." We don't believe we are wasting our money even though our rational mind knows that our chance of winning is nil. Managed funds don't beat the market most of the time. The odds are like those of a lottery—18 million to 1. Like the lottery, when we invest in a managed fund to "beat the market" we don't count up the costs of the "tickets." We may buy $25 worth of tickets a week and end up winning $1,000 in a year. We spent $1,200 for $1,000.

In the same manner, a mutual fund manager advertises that their fund has "beaten" the market and so we pay 1.5-3% of our assets every year. Over time we find that while the stock market index rose 11.11% for 30 years ended 2013, we earned only 3.69% annually. This is what happened to managed investment accounts, Dalbar's QAIB recent study showed.

Some of us keep switching to the hot stock/funds according to the advertising we see. Some are always chasing the last most successful stock/fund. Some buy the stock/fund at the high point because they want the winner. They sell when it falls and they want the next high flier. Over time they never earn the return promised by the manager/salesman.

In this way, costs can take 63% of their returns over time. Each time they sell and buy, they give up earnings and perhaps part of their money if they use a sales person charging 5%. Even if they stay with one managed mutual fund that has annual fees of 1.5-3%, they are killing the compounded earnings mechanism.

Using the compounding calculator, we can see that our accumulation drops to $473,000 if we earn 8% instead of 11% annually. We could have over $1 million in 34 years at 11%. http://www.moneychimp.com/calculator/compound_interest_calculator.htm

Another Wall Street myth is that investing in market index funds will produce average (mediocre) returns. It is true that the returns will be close to the returns of the market. However, historically the market returns are the ones that beat managed funds 80-90% overall. Investing in growing companies provides no guaranteed return but the average returns have held steady since the 1930s when they started keeping records. **See page 32**.

Wall Street history is littered with strategies that were said to beat the market. The brilliant stock pickers have also come and gone. Today, though, which one of the new ones are we going to invest with? No one knows. The ONLY thing we really know is that the averages of broad market indexes have produced 10-12% on average over time. See page 22.

For example, some of my clients use these Vanguard mutual funds which have earned over 11% for a long time. Of course, there is no guarantee of future returns, but they have all done fairly well. Most started with the 500 Index and added companies in the Energy, Health and International sectors. These 10 funds have done well over time. Many investors pick Vanguard funds because the funds are well run at cost. No "bells and whistles." No expensive managers and overhead. No owner taking profits from our investment returns.

2011 Total Return	Fund	Long-term Return*	Longevity
1.97%	500 Index	10.36%	since 1976
-1.74%	Energy	12.71%	since 1984
-3.73%	Extended Market Idx	9.96%	since 1987
11.45%	Health	16.30%	since 1984
-13.68%	International Growth	10.50%	since 1981
-1.84%	PRIMECAP	12.79%	since 1984
-2.80%	Small Cap Index	10.26%	since 1960
9.63%	Wellesley Income	10.16%	since 1970
-4.00%	Windsor	11.00%	since 1958
2.70%	Windsor II	10.18%	since 1985
0.00%	Average	11.42%	

*Average Annual Returns as of 12/31/11.

My clients are long-term investors, not speculators. They believe that investments in low-cost funds (index and managed) are their best chance of reaching their goals. They have been rewarded for that belief. Vanguard has many low-cost funds and their service is better than most fund firms.

Remember, we are investing for the long-term. Most pension funds are invested in stocks and bonds primarily. Even though the market fell 22% in 2002 and jumped 29% in 2003, the average was still holding. Average returns mean we do not suffer the lowest lows nor the highest highs. They "regress to the mean": 10-12%. This strategy is the closest we have to a certainty.

Most of the largest growing companies in the world are held by these funds. Large US firms are now earning at least **half of their profits overseas** so we are benefiting from growth around the world. This is important because we don't want to miss important earnings progress as the developing nations like China and India expand their economies.

We don't know exactly which companies will be winners but we want to participate in all of them. We want to own some smaller growing companies too. If they become successful, they will move to the large company funds. We are exposed to almost all areas of the global economy by buying shares of these mutual funds at the lowest cost. We suffer the ups and downs of the markets just like every investor. However, we see that some funds do better at certain times while others do worse. Together we see clients hitting their goal of 10-12% average annual returns.

This type of investing has the greatest chance of avoiding severe swings in the balance of our accumulation. This type of strategy—investing in different types and sizes of companies in different sectors around the world—is called Modern Portfolio Theory.

Modern Portfolio Theory

Some clients use the MPT strategy to control risk while increasing returns. MPT (Moneychimp.com/articles/risk/riskintro.htm) holds that if we put our eggs in different baskets of assets that grow at different times, then the value of all our eggs grows with fewer ups and downs. We can manage the ups and downs of equity funds by buying different ones over time. Higher risk assets are small caps, REITs and foreign stocks. This strategy earns 10-12% with 30% less volatility.

Members assemble asset classes (see http://www.callan.com/research/download/?file=periodic%2Ffree%2F757.pdf) that fit their risk-reward tastes. According to this Nobel Prize-winning strategy moneychimp.com/articles/risk/portfolio.htm, a high return asset with a low correlation to other assets in the portfolio can actually reduce the volatility of the whole. It may be possible to earn high returns with less risk **overall** as each asset goes up and down at different times. See the example at fool.com/personal-finance/retirement/2007/03/06/5-steps-to-salvage-your-retirement.aspx.

The past provides only PROBABLE futures. But isn't $1,000,000 (plus or minus $100,000) better than $200,000. Your $250-per-month deposit in a low-cost account for 33 years will be worth about $1 million from stock investing with no tax. Every investor would be better off with $1 million (+/- $100,000) than $200,000 from a high-cost account.

When clients begin investing, they cannot buy all 10 Vanguard funds at once with $250 per month. Vanguard has minimums on all funds so they can keep their expenses low for everyone.

There are two ways to start our **Wealth Reserve**™. The easiest way is to save $250 a month in our savings account until we have the $1,000 minimum for Vanguard's entry fund: STAR #56. We can open the Roth IRA by phone or online: STAR minimum is $1,000. Most Vanguard funds need $3,000 to start. We can keep contributing to this index fund until we have $3,000 for the 500 Index and then $3,000 for the Extended Market funds. Vanguard is at 800.551.8631.

The second way to begin is to open a Roth IRA at TIAA-CREF, the world's largest pension company, primarily for educational and research institutions. Low expenses and low initial contributions make TIAA-CREF an organization we can stay with for life. TIAA-CREF 800.842.2888.

At TIAA-CREF.org, we can make application and begin immediately with an automatic monthly contribution of $100 or more from our bank account. We can follow how the assets grow by themselves. TIAA-CREF has two funds that provide us with the diversity of companies worldwide: TIAA-CREF Equity Index and TIAA International Equity.

Request a prospectus (owner's manual) for each fund you will be using at Vanguard or TIAA-CREF. Both mutual fund firms have experienced salaried representatives that provide accurate information about accounts and funds. Both offer low-cost index funds that hold a broad representation of the market returns of 10-12%. This is a building block to accumulating wealth.

Both firms are focused on you, not on profits.

This strategy provides long-term growth of 10-12% annually on average with the benefit of avoiding single company or industry failures. It provides exposure to new growth potential around the world with less risk than holding one company, one sector, or one country. You don't have to give your sales person HALF your earnings. Your tax-FREE account adds another 20-30% to your total since there is no state or federal income tax. Pensions, IRAs and annuities are all taxable and may have high fees.

Create your highest retirement income not your broker's.

It is the amount we KEEP that matters!

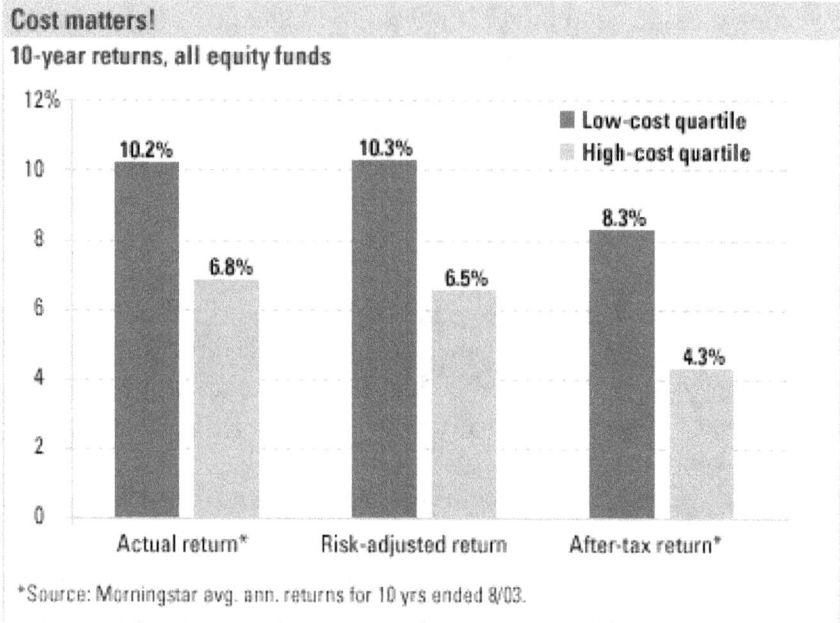

7

Expenses less than income

We create our future income by using a fraction of current income. We use $9 a day—$250 per month—to create $4,000 a month—$48,000 a year adjusted for inflation. We can build our **Wealth Reserve**™ of $1million by following the strategy outlined above.

We have to go back to our goal. We want to build wealth: accumulating $1,000,000 over time in order to have enough retirement income. Based on the way wealth compounds, we need at least $250 a month. We need to invest consistently for the power of compounding to work.

I want to explain how we can find the $250 a month to invest from a different perspective. If we are going to spend all of our income, we need to adopt a "spending plan" with the $250 a month for investment included in it. Otherwise, we won't accumulate $1,000,000. Even if we don't have 33 years, our $250 could grow to a significant sum.

A spending plan is just a way to set priorities for our regular spending. During our working lives, we earn about $1.5 to $2.5 million before taxes. We can accumulate another $1 million to accomplish all that we want to do in life by using just 10 percent of that income to buy assets that "grow by themselves."

Using a Spending Plan is **like brushing your teeth**—it's a habit that isn't that difficult to learn—then it is automatic. If we don't learn, our future is painful. Our plan becomes a habit when we practice it. If we consciously spend our income on those items on our priority list, we can't fail to develop the habit. We are teaching ourselves that we can have whatever we want **in time**. We are not saying "no" to that desire. We are saying put it on our list. We will get what we want eventually.

First, our Spending Plan must include what we need to function. Our future is part of our immediate needs in the sense that if we don't prepare now, we won't have the future we want.

Again, building a $1,000,000 **Wealth Reserve**™ is a lifelong process and requires making a commitment. Like building a business, it takes planning and following the steps we talked about so far.

There are a number of ways to identify the $250 a month we need to build our future. Some clients include the $250 in their automatic bill payment or have the trustee debit their account automatically. The contribution is just another bill like rent, mortgage, utilities, car payment, cable, phone, etc. They live on the balance of their income.

Others set up family goals and decide to put a certain amount in a separate account for each goal. In this way, they keep the wealth building process in the forefront of their monthly bill payments ritual.

Whatever way works for you. The important part is changing the status of wealth building from a vague future to a monthly priority.

Most clients find that the easiest way is to set up an automatic debit of their checking account by the trustee at the time of the application for the Roth IRA. If we are using a Roth 401k or other employer account, we set up the retirement account with automatic contributions.

The Spending Plan idea works for all types of goals: college fund, emergency fund, vacation fund, new car fund, business start-up fund, whatever we decide to put at the top of our list of priorities. If we don't have this list, we can make one easily.

Clients who are successful have made written plans in some form or other. They have some idea of how much they will need at some time in the future. For short-term goals we can use our savings account but for long-term goals we need to use higher return securities. Many clients have trouble deciding which investment to use for each goal.

I explain the chart we displayed on page 12 above. Stock mutual funds are the investment of choice for any long-term accumulation goal. As per the chart, annual returns of 10-12% are the norm for any accumulation over 5 years. Once we build up a sizable balance in a long-term account, we can "borrow" from ourselves for short-term needs as long as we pay ourselves back.

Thus, clients have used their long-term accumulation **Wealth Reserve**™ for vacations, cars, appliances, emergencies, etc. This works if they pay themselves back. The **Wealth Reserve**™ is set up as a Roth IRA so the *contributions* are not taxed when used before age 59.5. After that age, there are no taxes at all—EVER. However, to meet our long-term goals, we have to pay ourselves back quickly.

Another benefit of using a Spending Plan is that we become focused on how we spend our money. We are more inclined to buy only what we need. For most of us, when we shop for groceries, we seek to get the most for our money by shopping for discounts and by buying in bulk. In the last ten years, the financial services industry has started to offer better values on products. We can avoid paying the middle people and avoid buying products we really don't need. We buy what we need directly.

How do we learn? The ***Insiders Guides*** provide an easy way to save $3,000 or more on financial products we already use. There are buyer's guides for each specific area. We review some of the ways to find $250 in savings in the next chapter.

We can't build wealth by spending more than we earn. Building wealth takes patience and commitment to investing every month. Some people don't try to be disciplined investors. They let the trustee debit the $250 every month so they can't fail to invest. They use the **miracle of compounding** inside their low-cost tax-FREE account to turbocharge their $250 a month.

Your choice: **earn 11.11% or 3.69%**.

Are you paying too much?

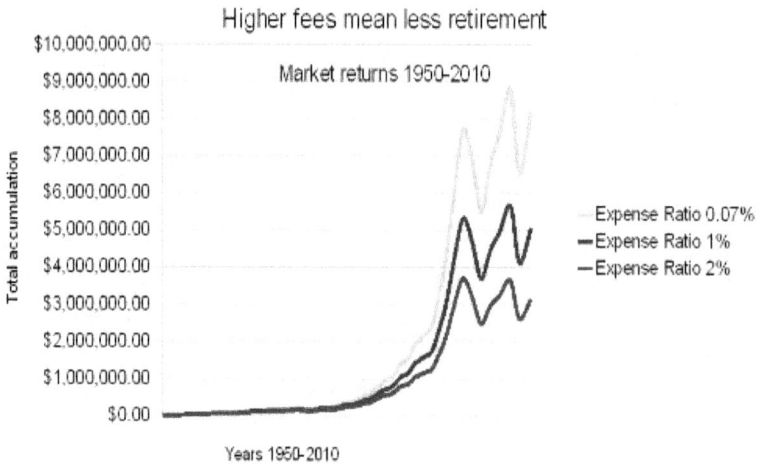

8

Buy only services you need

Every $100 invested, not wasted, is worth $4,000 later.

It is easy to build wealth if we already have a pile of money. It takes 6-9 years to accumulate $1 million if you already have $500,000. But how do we capture that first $250,000, that first $100,000, or even that first $50,000? It comes from buying assets that 'grow by themselves.' It takes time and the easiest way to make sure we reach our goal is to make our monthly contributions automatic.

But where do we get the $250 or more? The best way is to "REDIRECT" the **cash we already spend** on things we really don't need or can buy for less.

Monthly	Accumulation at 12% per year									
	5	10	15	20	25	30	35	40	45	50
$100	$8,167	$23,004	$49,958	$98,925	$187,884	$349,496	$643,095	$1,176,477	$2,145,469	$3,905,834
$200	$16,334	$46,008	$99,916	$197,850	$375,768	$698,992	$1,286,190	$2,352,954	$4,290,938	$7,811,668
$300	$24,501	$69,012	$149,874	$296,775	$563,652	$1,048,488	$1,929,285	$3,529,431	$6,436,408	$11,717,502
$500	$40,835	$115,020	$249,790	$494,625	$939,420	$1,747,480	$3,215,475	$5,882,385	$10,727,346	$19,529,169

While working with clients, I have found that most of us **waste $3,000 or more each year** on financial services. We can stop paying for services we don't need. This takes a little thought and questioning on our part, but in reality it is the same process as buying any commodity. When we buy groceries, do we buy the house brand or the one on sale or the one we see advertised? On a little bigger scale, do we buy the new car advertised with a new "push" starter as opposed to an old key-type ignition? Do we pay an extra $1000 to buy the one with a screen to tell us where to go or just buy a map? The difference between paying full price for a new car and a 3-year-old model with fewer gadgets can be 40% or more. When we put our future on top of our priority list, we can REDIRECT the savings to a more worthwhile purpose.

It is the same with financial services. Most of us are not used to shopping for insurance, mutual funds, banking and mortgages. So we don't. We are operating under the mythology of Wall Street —'professionals' say we need them to help guide us, for a price. But we don't need them anymore. The world has changed.

Let's take some examples of **annual savings**:

Auto insurance: save $400 or more EVERY year by changing/dropping some benefits we don't need.

Home insurance: save $200 or more EVERY year by changing one limit.

Life insurance: save $1,000 or more EVERY year by using direct to consumer insurer.

Mutual funds: save $2-3,000 EVERY year by using low-cost providers.

Bank: save $120 EVERY year by using a low-cost provider of the benefits we usually use.

Mortgage: save $2,000 on closings and lower interest rates.

Investments: earn 15-30% guaranteed just by paying off credit cards.

Tax refund: Averages $3,022 for investing the easy way.

Using the Insiders' Guides put together by Dan Keppel in *The Insiders' Guides to Buying Discount Financial Services: Buy Direct and Save $3,000 Every Year,* we can REDIRECT the $250 a month without having to give up anything. We don't need to tighten our belt or make a budget. We can give up things we would not benefit from anyway. amazon.com/gp/product/143480593X

Dan gave me a number of stories from people who have told him about their experience using the Guides.

George B. New York:
"I saved $1,356 on my vehicle insurance using your Insider's Guide to Vehicle Insurance. I saved by using some of your Insiders' 'tricks of the trade' like dropping the extras that I already had."

John D. New York:
"I canceled my life insurance and used the money to buy the mutual funds. You were right. I didn't need the insurance anymore. My kids are all grown. My new wife and I invest as much as we can now. Your Guide to 'Living' Insurance is a great way to look at

our insurance needs."

Mark K. Ohio:
"I had no idea how to invest in the 401k that my new job offered. I have not been disappointed with the mutual funds suggested by other members. I saved about a $1,000 by transferring my old 401k mutual funds to the low-cost funds in your Guide. When I sold my primary residence in 2004, I followed members' advice with the gains. I use all your Guides to help me save more for my retirement since I got a late start. Thanks."

Dan has a great example of the big savings we can expect by shopping for insurance. Dan found that people usually pick name brands instead of shopping for services they need. Companies spend a lot for TV advertising, agents and gimmicks we pay for.
Example:
MetLife charged $983 for a $300,000 30-year **term policy**. This same $300,000 benefit was sold by Savings Bank Life Insurance for $384 a year. Their financial strength ratings are A+ and their underwriting requirements are the same. The difference, $599, over 30 years is $17,970. If invested, this difference can add $175,000 to OUR **Wealth Reserve**™.

Most people are amazed at the difference a little research and shopping can accomplish. Even if we did not have Dan's *Guides*, a search of the Internet would reveal several portals that quote rates. Unfortunately, most people don't take the time to shop or don't know exactly what they need. The *Guides* help us make the decision of where to shop and what to buy.

Buying only what we need in every financial service area will provide the cash for our tax-FREE account contributions. Taking the time to shop in each area of our expenses helps us make our future happen. Shopping for an hour can add $175,000 to our account.

Yes, it is worth it! *We give up nothing and create our future retirement income.*

The Roth IRA Rules

Contributions:

$5,500 ($6,500 over age 50) each year
Income under $129,000 (2014) single
$191,000 married (2014)

Distributions:

Tax-FREE for contributions.
And Tax-FREE for earnings if
Over age 59 1/2,
Account open 5 years,
Taxable earnings unless
Disabled,
First home ($10,000),
Death

Bonus:

Account can grow tax-FREE for life
No forced withdrawals at age 71
Heirs don't pay income tax
Account has no maximum

Check with your tax preparer
www.IRS.gov/pub/irs-pdf/p590.pdf

9

Leave it alone

*"We continue to make more money when **snoring** than when active."*

Warren Buffett

This is the advice of the most successful investor of our day. He is making it clear that we should NOT touch our investments very often. Contrary to the advice of the Wall Street 'professionals,' he leaves his assets alone to compound over time. He does not follow the 'hot' investment of the day. He buys the stock of growing companies around the world. He has held some investments like Coke for over 40 years.

Our emotions tell us to sell when our account balance goes down. We want to buy the next big investment to make up for previous losses. This is why we have a hard time following Buffett's advice. However, the emotions that cause us to be bad investors are what we can control—not the stock price of growing companies worldwide.

Our contributions to our **Wealth Reserve**™ need to be automatic so we buy more shares when the market is down and less when it is up. This helps us control our emotions. When the market is down, we need to look at the line graph on page 16. We don't know when the market will be up or down but we see that if we sell, we may miss the next advance. This is why we have to remember Warren Buffett's advice and hold on to stocks. In fact, Mr Buffett says **"our favorite holding period is forever."** http://www.berkshirehathaway.com/letters/1988.html

When we own a broad cross-section of the market, we really don't have to worry about buying and selling our mutual funds. There is no better investment for the long term. Besides, what would we buy if we sold? We have seen that stock funds are the safest investment for periods over 10 years.

We have learned that the only way to avoid bad investment decisions is to NOT make any investment decisions in haste. Stick with the idea that we only have to look at our tax-FREE account once a year. At that time, I make sure I am making contributions to the specific mutual fund I need to build in order to keep them equally funded.

For instance, when I first started investing, I used the 500 Index. After I had accumulated enough to buy the Extended Market, I sold shares of 500 Index ($3,000) and bought it. I kept investing into the 500 Index until I had the minimum for the next one on the list. I repeated this pattern until I had the minimum in each. Then I picked one to add $250 a month for one year. The next year, I did the same until I completed the list again and again.

Today, I am still making contributions using the same rotation. Once a year, I compare the total account balance to where I think it should be. I note what happened during the year for any one fund. I go to the Vanguard site and read about that fund. Do I need to make a change? No, usually I don't. I only use the 10 funds listed above. They have done well consistently over the years.

Notice that when we buy each fund at first, we have to sell shares in the 500 Index to do so. Because we are using a Roth IRA, there is no tax on this sale if the share price has gone up. Also, each year, our dividends are re-invested without paying tax on that income. This is part of the miracle of compounding. Our account is growing without taxes each year. Any other non-retirement account would be diminished by the tax paid each year.

There is no need to sell funds that have done well in order to re-balance the 10 funds' balances equally. Most of the research shows that re-balancing each year does not change the long-term outcome of the whole portfolio. Some clients use their contributions each year to add to the fund that has grown the least. However, as each fund becomes larger, the effect of adding contributions becomes smaller over time.

When we have to sell shares to meet an emergency or avoid interest payments by using cash for large ticket items, we may sell shares in each fund by equal dollar amounts. This is a better strategy than selling shares in only one fund since we don't know which fund may recover the fastest going forward. In the same way as accumulating shares, we need to reimburse our account for the amount used. It is very desirable to also continue to make contributions at the regular rate—$250 per month. This way we are assured of catching up to our position as we reach our goal.

However, we found that after accumulating a large proportion of our goal, adding the $250 per month did not seem to matter to the outcome. For instance, our client whose account is shown on page 22 took $25,000 for a used luxury car in the year the account hit over half a million. He also stopped making contributions. His account total did not suffer long term.

Actually this client redirected his $250 monthly contribution to his grandchild's **Wealth Reserve**™ so that they might have a financial foundation all their life. If he keeps giving this $3,000 a year to his offspring for 40 years, they could have $2,000,000 by age 50. The grandchild "earns" $3,000 a year doing odd jobs for him. Learn more about this "Gift of a Lifetime" in Dan Keppel's book, amazon.com/Give-your-Grandchild-000-Lifetime/.

Our tax-FREE account does not require us to hire an advisor to manage it. Advisors do not know what the future holds anymore than we do so paying them 1-3% each year just reduces our annual returns. Their fees/charges can take up to 63% of our total accumulations over time.

We are investing for the long term and there is no proof that switching from one fund to another during the year does anything to help our results. As we add more contributions, we can rotate through each fund we use. The less we tamper with our fund balances the better our experience will be. Our tax-FREE low-cost account works best when we let *compounding compound* our investment earnings.

The irony is that by doing *nothing* after we set up our automatic investment plan, we create higher income for our future.

Our choice: **$80,000 or $20,000**.

Your Action Plan

This week:
Goal

Start Roth IRA fund for each of us

This month:
Goal

Re-direct expenses: cut what we don't need or can buy for less

This year:
Goals

Transfer all mutual funds to low-cost provider

Switch 401k 403b funds to stock index funds

Future Goals

Retire on $80,000 a year

_____
_____
_____
_____
_____
_____
_____

10

Tax-FREE income

We have used the 10 steps of building our low-cost account. We have learned to be patient and accumulate $1,000,000 or more. We have paid back any amounts that we borrowed to pay cash for large purchases. We have been fortunate that the historical averages of market returns have produced the accumulations we wanted.

NOW WHAT?

Now we can take $80,000 out of the account each year and pay no income taxes. As of 2014, most states follow the IRS code on our **Wealth Reserve**™, a Roth IRA—§ 408 trust account.
http://www.irs.gov/retirement/article/0,,id=137307,00.html

Some clients move some of their accumulations into a bond fund in order to provide a monthly check to their checking account for fixed expenses like an annuity. They created a retirement spending plan that assured them of that monthly income of a fixed dollar amount with this Guide. amazon.com/Your-Retirement-Spending-Plan-enough

We have to create our $1,000,000 nest egg in order to provide the same buying power as we have today because of inflation. I am assuming that most families will need at least $60,000 a year to live on in retirement. We don't know how much Social Security will pay later. We don't know what employer pensions might look like by then. I am assuming that inflation will continue at a 3% rate. It might be more or less. I have no idea. However, we must prepare for inflation.

At 3%, inflation will make the goods we buy now for $50,000 cost about $80,000. This is not exact. I don't know what will happen in 40 days let alone 40 years. Social Security and employer pensions can add $20,000 to our basic income. But we don't want to count on them. http://www.fool.com/retirement/general/2014/10/12/what-the-retirement-calculators-wont-tell-you.aspx

I am using $50,000 as a basic needs income because that has been my experience of what working people desire. It is also an amount that could be generated by our $1,000,000 account balance. Many clients use 6-8% as a target for their investment returns in retirement. This is just an approximation of the average returns over time. Most people add Social Security and other income.

Some clients move some of their money into a balanced fund in order to provide the income for the coming year. The balance of their account remains in the broad stock funds we have listed above. These funds will continue to produce returns in the 10-12% range. If there is a bad year like 2008, we are not taking money out of our principal at a bad time. We cut back on our expenses instead.

The funds we have listed above include some of the most consistent low volatility returns over time. The <u>Wellesley Income</u> fund has produced **over 10% per year** on average since 1970. It contains stocks and bonds. **This fund alone might be our source** of annual withdrawals of <u>principal and dividends</u>. Since this account is not taxable, there are no tax considerations in the decision of which fund to tap for our monthly income.

Because we have no tax liability on this income, we may not have to pay tax on our other income like Social Security and/or our qualified retirement funds. 85% of Social Security benefits are currently subject to federal income taxes. The IRS <u>worksheet</u> determines the percentage based on all our other income. Typically those with little or no other income currently have no tax due on their Social Security benefits. Pensions are taxed as income not capital gains since we did not pay tax on all the contributions.

In most cases, we will pay little income tax on our income in retirement since the bulk of it will be tax-FREE. This will give us 25-30% more cash to spend compared with others who do not have the **Wealth Reserve**™. Pensions and other taxable income may be taxed at even higher rates in the future to pay for the two wars and two tax cuts that we endured since 2001. We have never gone to war and taken tax breaks at the same time before so this will take time for Americans to pay off.

Our tax-FREE income will provide us with our basic-needs income and if we continue to follow the same 10 steps of building wealth, we will find a comfortable lifestyle throughout the 30 to 40 years of not working unless we want to.

Many clients and I are <u>assuming we will work</u> at least part time after we take full retirement and begin collecting Social Security. If benefits are cut, we will need to work. We are encouraged to use our tax-FREE income to develop a small business since this can help us control the income that is taxed. irs.gov/Businesses/Tax-Credits

As I mentioned at the beginning of this book, many working millionaires are self-employed. Running a small business is a great way to control the taxes they pay. Taxes are the biggest killer of wealth building that exists. It destroys the compounding factor.

The accumulation of $1,000,000 over time can be achieved with patience and perseverance. Spending the income that $1,000,000 can generate may require us to take some principal from time to time. If we use the same 10 steps of wealth building to do this, we will probably have enough to take care of long-term health care and other unforeseen expenses. Since we don't know what may happen, we will want to continue the same spending habits we have developed before retirement. We live within our means and own stock funds.

We may find that we will have a sizable legacy as we age. There are many ways to pass on our wealth that don't require an attorney on contingency or complicated legal formulations. Many clients have found that incremental gifts to charity and family provide immediate gratification. They have used the suggestions for wealth transfer Dan Keppel presented in the ***Retirement Spending Plan***.

Most of your income will be tax-FREE. You avoid the increase in taxes to pay for past bad decisions—two wars and two tax cuts. Working millionaires typically don't go out and buy a mansion and the trappings of the wealthy when they retire. They usually have paid off their homes. They travel and share with family. Some continue to earn income doing what they enjoy or provide help to others in their volunteer efforts.

You use your low-cost tax-FREE account for income and avoid the taxes on pensions, IRAs, and annuities. You may have 30% more money to spend too.

Spend $80,000 or $20,000. Your choice!

How to Buy Securities for Retirement

1.   Cost matters: Broker/advisor cost 1% to 3%

If you use a salesperson, costs take HALF your money!
$3,000 per year @11%   for 33 years = $1,018,177
$3,000 per year @11-1% for 33 years = $778,768
$3,000 per year @11-2% for 33 years = $613,805
$3,000 per year @11-3% for 33 years = $486,634
www.moneychimp.com/calculator/compound_interest_calculator.htm

2. Broker/advisor stock picking does not beat index funds over the long run. No money manager has been able to beat the market consistently. No one can forecast the future.

3. Time is the key to investment success. The chance of you buying AND selling, both, at the right times, is near zero.

4. A Tax-FREE investment account increases your balance 25%.

5. Putting all your money in one stock or market sector guarantees failure over time. No one investment is perfect but low cost is the best predictor of successful investing.

6. 'Dollar cost average' buying technique lowers the cost of shares over time. When you invest a fixed amount each month, you buy more mutual fund shares when the price is low and less when high. Over time, you will own more shares at a lower average cost.

7. **Earn more**—Use low-cost stock funds inside a special tax-FREE account—there is no better investment.

Spend $80,000 or $20,000 a year

Invest $9 a day for $80,000 or $20,000 a year—your choice

You can shop and save on your insurance, banking and investing. You buy quality and keep more of your earnings. You avoid taxes in your special IRS-approved tax shelter. You can't use Google's tax dodges—the "Double Irish" and the "Dutch Sandwich"—to pay 2.4%. But you CAN build $1,000,000 with ZERO tax. You don't need to give up $400,000 in fees to an advisor. You don't need broker stock picks or high-cost mutual funds offered by a sales person. Buy the low-cost Vanguard funds by phone.
    Check out what I have suggested using unbiased sources. Confirm for yourself that compounding high earnings inside your tax shelter is your best chance of avoiding the taxes that are needed to pay off 2 wars and 2 tax breaks that helped the '1 percenters.'
    My industry is not going to help you. They tell you that you need them: a "doctor" of financial health who is overpaid. The industry takes $560 billions from investors' accounts year after year with limited improvement over low-cost funds. Trading stocks without insider info does NOT benefit you. pbs.org/moyers/journal/09282007/
    It is simple math. If you pay 1-3% of your nest egg every year to your advisor, you are going to get less. No advisor can beat the market over time. That $3-5,000 a year in fees is really paying the Wall Street Wolf. Over time that fee goes up as you invest more and can take up to 63% of your possible total. Advisors like to buy and sell securities creating taxes and fees that don't help you.
    The key to reaching our goal is compounding of high returns over time. If we pay 2% to get 10-12%, we net 8-10%. Since we know that no advisor can guarantee 10-12% and most studies show investing directly without a "professional" can yield the same result, there is no reason to give up 2%. Advisors usually charge 1-2% whether they beat the averages or not so it is better to go for the 10-12% on our own. Salespeople **don't give refunds**!
    The clear winning strategy is to use Warren Buffett's strategy

of compounding. Over time using a tax-FREE account without an advisor fee, you can accumulate $1,000,000 from $250 a month at 10-12%. Using a compounding calculator like this one, http://www.moneychimp.com/calculator/compound_interest_calculator.htm, we find the range is about 33 years. If you and your spouse each have an account, you can double it—$2 million.

If you use an advisor, you may give up over $400,000 in total accumulation. Research has shown that the average investor actually earns about **3.69%** annually over time. ETFguide.com

Our 10 steps of building wealth succeed because they are straightforward strategies using a unique **tax-FREE trust account** that eliminates the biggest killer of wealth: TAXES. We have seen that compounding over time is the real engine for building wealth. Most people are NOT going to be successful at this because they have no patience to let compounding do the work.

We can be our own masters of tax-FREE wealth with patience. There is no need to pick stocks or hire expensive advisors or product pushers with hidden fees. We can do it ourselves without the middle person. Our best chance to succeed is to have a plan with low-cost investments. The plan can be set up in 1 hour:

1. Create a $1,000,000 tax-FREE accumulation.
2. Use a tax-favored lifetime investment account.
3. Compound high earnings.
4. Automate monthly contributions.
5. Use low-cost mutual funds.
6. Buy a large group of stocks of growing companies worldwide.
7. Keep expenses less than income.
8. Buy only the financial services you need.
9. Manage the account only once a year.
10. Take tax-FREE income each year.

You must take the first step. **I don't have a product to sell** you so I won't be calling you. You have to call Vanguard 800.551.8631 or TIAA-CREF 800.842.2888 yourself to set up your account. It takes about an hour to set up a Roth IRA for each of you. You can do it online or by phone. You can begin with TIAA-CREF and $100 automatic contributions or Vanguard with $1,000. Put the contributions on automatic so you don't have to decide every month whether to invest. That is usually how people fail. Life happens and there is always an emergency that requires cash. But your future life happens too and you both want to be spending your $6,000 a month not praying the government won't cut Social Security benefits every year.

There is a clear reason why the <u>working millionaires</u> become wealthy. It is not luck or inheritance. Millions of immigrants to this country have done it before. They lived below their means. They saved and invested in businesses they understood. They did not let temporary cash flow problems stop them from building wealth. They used the 10 steps of building wealth every day.

As many clients say, "I never even miss the contributions because I never see them. Then all of a sudden, I see my statement has $25,000, $50,000, $250,000, $500,000. We are talking real money here."

You have done the numbers
Now,
Create the retirement income you desire

Go tax-FREE using a special low-cost investment account. Your advisor already uses one so they will understand when you switch and invest by yourself.

Tax-FREE Wealth is a habit not a lottery.

Call Vanguard 800.551.8631 or TIAA-CREF 800.842.2888 today.

Let me know how you do:
IANBooksEditor@yahoo.com

NOTES

The Author

Ian Sender has been a financial services executive for over 20 years. He was a managing director of sales units of securities firms. He is one of the Insiders who contributed to the ***The Insiders Guides*** set of buyers' guides edited by Dan Keppel. The guides provide specific ways to save on all financial services. ***The Insiders' Guides to Buying Discount Financial Services: Buy Direct and Save $3,000 Every Year*** is available at Amazon, Barnes and Noble, Abebooks. Ian lives in New Jersey and the Caymans.

To receive Dan Keppel's weekly Alert of saving ideas, go to www.TheInsidersGuides.com or his blog at http://dankeppel.blogspot.com/

www.ingramcontent.com/pod-product-compliance
Lightning Source LLC
Chambersburg PA
CBHW071803200526
45167CB00017B/1231